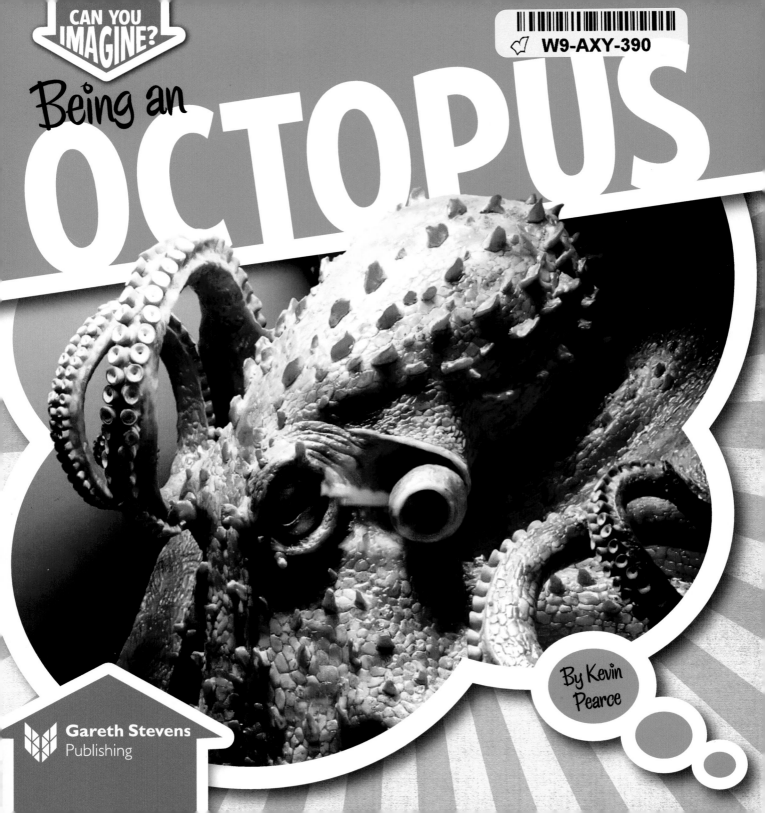

CAN YOU IMAGINE?

Being an
OCTOPUS

W9-AXY-390

By Kevin Pearce

Gareth Stevens
Publishing

Please visit our website, www.garethstevens.com. For a free color catalog of all our high-quality books, call toll free 1-800-542-2595 or fax 1-877-542-2596.

Library of Congress Cataloging-in-Publication Data

Pearce, Kevin.
Being an octopus / by Kevin Pearce.
 p. cm. — (Can you imagine?)
Includes index.
ISBN 978-1-4824-3281-7 (pbk.)
ISBN 978-1-4824-3282-4 (6-pack)
ISBN 978-1-4824-0136-3 (library binding)
1. Octopuses — Juvenile literature. I. Pearce, Kevin. II. Title.
QL430.3.O2 P43 2014
594.56—dc23

First Edition

Published in 2014 by
**Gareth Stevens Publishing**
111 East 14th Street, Suite 349
New York, NY 10003

Copyright © 2014 Gareth Stevens Publishing

Designer: Katelyn E. Reynolds
Editor: Therese Shea

Photo credits: Cover, p. 1 Dieter H/Shutterstock.com; cover, pp. 1–32 (background texture) AnnabelleaDesigns/Shutterstock.com; pp. 4, 14 Hemera/Thinkstock.com; pp. 5, 13 iStockphoto/Thinkstock.com; p. 7 (inset) Douglas Klung/Flickr/Getty Images; p. 7 (main) Wolfgang Poelzer/WaterFrame/Getty Images; p. 9 mj007/Shutterstock.com; p. 11 kangarooarts/Shutterstock.com; p. 15 Rich Carey/Shutterstock.com; p. 16 Isantilli/Shutterstock.com; p. 17 (inset) Gary Ombler/Dorling Kindersley/Getty Images; p. 17 (main) © iStockphoto.com/Angelafoto; p. 18 Geoff Brightling/Dorling Kindersley/Getty Images; p. 19 Teguh Tirtaputra/Shutterstock.com; p. 20 Don Farrall/Stone/Getty Images; pp. 21, 29 Vittorio Bruno/Shutterstock.com; p. 23 FAUP/Shutterstock.com; p. 25 Joe Belanger/Shutterstock.com; pp. 26, 27 Robert F. Sisson/National Geographic/Getty Images; p. 28 surabhi25/Shutterstock.com.

Printed in the United States of America

CPSIA compliance information: Batch #CW14GS: For further information contact Gareth Stevens, New York, New York at 1-800-542-2595.

# CONTENTS

Words in the glossary appear in **bold** type the first time they are used in the text.

# EIGHT-ARMED WONDER

What would you do if you had eight arms? Would you become an incredible drummer? Would you be the fastest chef in the world? An octopus's amazing eight arms are one of the key **adaptations** that help it survive in the ocean.

Octopuses are invertebrates, which means they don't have a backbone. In fact, if you were an octopus, you wouldn't have any bones at all! Can you imagine your body without bones? You'd be a blob, just like an octopus!

## imagine that!

"Octopus" comes from a Greek word that means "eight-footed."

Octopuses are different sizes and colors, but all have eight arms.

5

# BIG AND SMALL

If you were an octopus, would you want to be very tiny or really huge? The smallest octopuses are less than 1 inch (2.5 cm) long. The largest grow more than 20 feet (6.1 m) long.

Scientists have counted about 250 kinds, or species, of octopuses so far. However, there may be more. Some octopuses live so far out in the ocean that they're hard to study. Others live in warm, shallow waters near the coasts.

## imagine that!

The largest giant Pacific octopus ever found measured 30 feet (9.1 m) long! Most are smaller, though.

giant Pacific octopus

The California octopus is the smallest species, and the giant Pacific octopus is the largest.

California octopus

7

# WEIRD BODY

Can you imagine if your head were attached to your legs? Octopuses are part of a group of **mollusks** called cephalopods (SEH-fuh-luh-pahdz). That word means "head-foot." An octopus's head is attached to its feet (or arms).

An octopus has a soft bag-like head. Attached are its eight strong arms, each with two rows of "suckers." These suckers help the octopus to stick to surfaces, hold things, and move along the bottom of the ocean. They're also how an octopus touches and tastes.

## imagine that!

Scientists think that each octopus arm works by itself. The brain sends an order, and each arm decides how to carry out the order.

Each octopus arm can have as many as 200 suckers.

9

# SHELL-LESS

The mollusk group also includes clams and snails. What do these sea creatures have that octopuses don't? Shells! Luckily, octopuses have many other ways to keep themselves safe from predators.

Instead of having a hard shell for **protection** like other mollusks, the octopus's soft body can fit into holes to avoid danger. You'd be surprised how large octopuses can hide in small places! Octopus arms are also very strong, even without any bones. How strong? If you were a large octopus, you could **wrestle** a shark!

## imagine that!

Octopuses have **gills** to breathe.

This octopus hides out in a pot that fell to the ocean floor.

11

# CAMOUFLAGED!

Octopuses have an even better trick. They can **camouflage** themselves! Octopuses change the color and pattern of their skin so they're very hard to see.

Because octopuses don't have bones, they can shape their bodies to look like many different objects, including other sea animals and plants. Hungry predators won't see them or will think they're another kind of animal and just keep swimming by. Would you want to be like an octopus in this way?

## imagine that!

Even though octopuses can change color, scientists don't think they can see colors well!

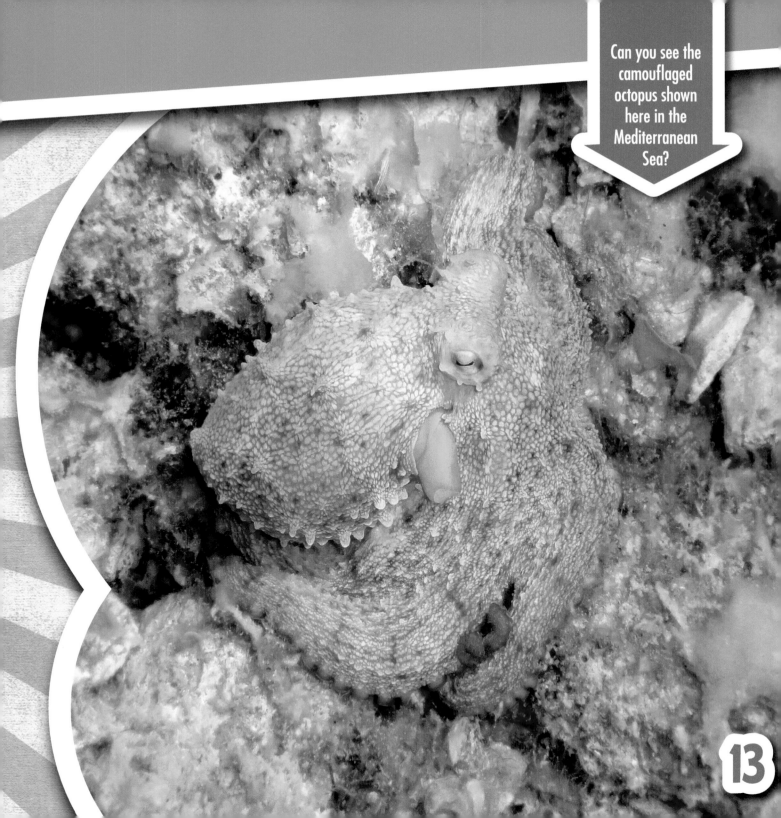

Can you see the camouflaged octopus shown here in the Mediterranean Sea?

13

# GETTING AROUND

If you were an octopus, you'd find a new home every week or so! Octopus dens aren't very fancy. They're usually under a rock, in a crack, or any other place they can hide their bodies.

Octopuses come out at night to hunt. They like to walk with their arms on the seafloor. If an octopus needs to move fast, it takes in water and then blows it out with great force. This pushes the octopus in the opposite direction.

## imagine that!

Octopuses can move through the water at 25 miles (40 km) per hour!

This octopus takes a stroll along the ocean floor while looking for a snack!

15

# A BITE TO EAT

What are your favorite foods? If you love to eat fish, clams, crabs, and lobsters, you might want to be an octopus! These are some of their favorite prey. Octopuses can reach into small places with their boneless arms to grab their prey.

An octopus doesn't have teeth. Instead, it has a sharp **beak** inside its mouth. The beak can crack shells. The octopus also has a special tongue that can scrape food out of shells.

## imagine that!

Octopuses also have a mouthpart that works like a drill in case its beak doesn't do the job!

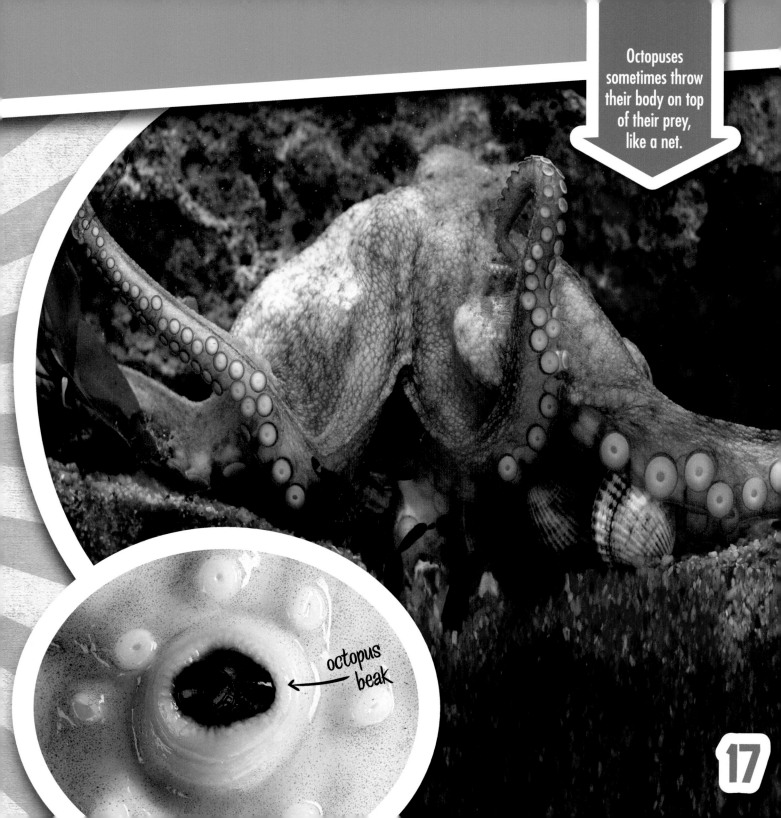

Octopuses sometimes throw their body on top of their prey, like a net.

octopus beak

17

# POISON!

Octopuses may grab prey that can grab them back, such as lobsters. They have a **weapon** for this. If you were an octopus, you'd be **venomous**! When an octopus bites its prey, venom in its spit enters the prey and stops it from moving. Venom also breaks down food so it's easier to eat.

If you were the blue-ringed octopus, you'd be the deadliest of all. Once a person is bitten by one of these, the venom can stop their breathing. People can die from the venom's effects if not treated in time.

model of a blue-ringed octopus showing its insides

The blue-ringed octopus's venom isn't made in its own body. Instead, it's made by **bacteria** living inside its body!

# INKED

As an octopus, you'd have a lot of enemies, even with your venomous bite. Octopuses' predators include eels, otters, seals, and even large fish like halibut and barracuda. Luckily, octopuses have a few more tricks!

Octopuses can squirt an inky liquid into the water. The ink makes a black cloud and hides the octopus until it can escape. The ink can also affect a predator's sense of smell and taste, so it can't locate the octopus that way.

## imagine that!

If a predator attacks an octopus's arm, the octopus may leave the arm behind. It can grow a new one later!

An octopus's ink cloud may look like another sea creature to a predator.

21

# A BRAINY CREATURE

If you were an octopus, you'd be pretty brainy. In fact, octopuses are the smartest invertebrates in the world. At least one kind, the veined octopus, is part of the small group of animals that use tools. The veined octopus has been spotted collecting coconut and clam shells to use later for protection!

Octopuses "play," which is a sign of **intelligence**. Some kinds can open jars and figure out how to get through mazes. Aquariums give their octopuses puzzles to work on.

## imagine that!

Scientists have found out that octopuses have memories, just like people do!

Other animals that use tools besides the octopus are sea otters, some kinds of birds, chimpanzees, and people!

# WALKING ON TWO LEGS

Even though you'd have eight arms as an octopus, you might use two of them as legs. At least two species walk on the ocean floor using their back two arms. The other six arms are used to grab objects and perform other functions. That makes the octopus the only animal in the oceans that walks on two legs!

Walking this way helps an octopus keep its camouflage while still moving. One kind of octopus that can camouflage itself to look like **algae** can walk without changing its shape.

## imagine that!

Octopuses can stretch their arms to twice their normal length!

This coconut octopus walks while carrying a shell for protection.

25

# BABY OCTOPUSES

If you were an octopus, you'd begin life in an egg. You'd have a large family. The mother octopus lays thousands of eggs in a den to keep them safe. She blows water at them because they need **oxygen**. She spends so much time taking care of her eggs that she doesn't eat. When the eggs hatch, the mother octopus dies.

Baby octopuses are on their own. Most are eaten by fish and other sea creatures before they reach adulthood.

octopus guards eggs →

Even the largest octopuses start out as babies about the size of a grain of rice!

# SHORT, DANGEROUS LIFE

Though an octopus has many tricks—from squirting ink to camouflaging its skin—it lives quite a dangerous underwater life. Even if octopuses survive to become fully grown, most live only a year or two. Even giant Pacific octopuses only live 5 years at most.

The ocean is a place full of predators, even for a fierce creature like the octopus. So do you think you'd like to be an octopus? It might be safer just to keep reading about them!

# Eight Fascinating Octopus Facts

- A male octopus may remove one of his arms and give it to a female.

- A female octopus may eat her mate.

- Octopuses have three hearts.

- Only about 2 out of 57,000 giant Pacific octopuses will grow to adulthood.

- Octopuses have blue blood.

- Some kinds of octopuses have two fins on their head that help them swim.

- Octopuses have been known to make a rock "door" for their den.

- Mimic octopuses are so smart that they shape themselves to look like fish and sea snakes that would be scary to their predators.

# GLOSSARY

**adaptation:** a change in a type of animal that makes it better able to live in its surroundings

**algae:** living plantlike things that are mostly found in water

**bacteria:** tiny creatures that can only be seen with a microscope

**beak:** a hard part of the mouth that sticks out on some animals and is used to tear food

**camouflage:** using colors or shapes to blend in with surroundings

**gill:** the body part that ocean animals such as fish and octopuses use to breathe in water

**intelligence:** the ability to learn skills and apply them

**mollusk:** an animal that lacks a backbone and has a soft body, such as a snail, clam, or octopus

**oxygen:** a colorless, odorless gas that most animals, including people, need to breathe

**protection:** the act of keeping safe

**venomous:** able to produce a liquid called venom that is harmful to other animals

**weapon:** something used to fight an enemy

**wrestle:** to fight by gripping, holding, and pushing rather than hitting

# FOR MORE INFORMATION

## Books

Claybourne, Anna. *Octopuses*. Chicago, IL: Capstone Raintree, 2014.

Gray, Leon. *Giant Pacific Octopus: The World's Largest Octopus*. New York, NY: Bearport Publishing, 2013.

Spilsbury, Louise. *Octopus*. Chicago, IL: Heinemann Library, 2011.

## Websites

**Giant Pacific Octopus**
*www.neaq.org/animals_and_exhibits/animals/giant_pacific_octopus/*
Learn much more about the fascinating giant Pacific octopus.

**How Octopuses Work**
*science.howstuffworks.com/zoology/marine-life/octopus.htm*
Find out many interesting facts about different kinds of octopuses.

# INDEX